M is for Mount Rushmore

A South Dakota Alphabet

Written by William Anderson and Illustrated by Cheryl Harness

Sleeping Bear Press™
2395 South Huron Parkway, Suite 200
Ann Arbor, MI 48104
www.sleepingbearpress.com

Printed and bound in the United States.

10 9 8 7 6

Library of Congress Cataloging-in-Publication Data

Anderson, William
M is for Mount Rushmore : a South Dakota alphabet / by William Anderson;
illustrated by Cheryl Harness.
p. cm.
Summary: "An A-Z pictorial for children all about South Dakota including
famous people, geography, history, and state symbols. Topics are introduced
with poems accompanied by expository text to provide detailed information"
—Provided by publisher.
ISBN 978-1-58536-141-0
1. South Dakota—Juvenile literature. 2. English language—Alphabet—Juvenile
literature. I. Harness, Cheryl, ill. II. Title.
F651.3.A535 2005
978.3—dc22   2004027296

For all my friends in the great state of South Dakota,
past and present.

WILLIAM

❧

To the memory of a great lady, Laura Ingalls Wilder,
who planted South Dakota into my imagination.
And to the author of this book, who taught the world about her.

CHERYL

South Dakota's first artists were Sioux tribes. Examples of their brightly beaded moccasins, decorated drums, and painted buffalo hide robes can be seen in South Dakota museums. Today Native American artists still create art, inspired by tribal traditions.

Harvey Dunn (1884–1952) was born near Manchester, South Dakota. He became a successful painter, illustrator, and teacher early in the twentieth century. In his studio in Tenafly, New Jersey and on visits to South Dakota, he painted hundreds of scenes of pioneer life on the prairie. Two of his best-loved paintings in South Dakota are "Something for Supper" and "The Prairie Is My Garden." In 1950 Dunn gave many of his original canvases to his home state. They are on exhibit in the South Dakota Art Museum in Brookings.

Oscar Howe (1915–1983) was a Sioux painter who combined modern art techniques with pictures of traditional Native American life. His paintings are displayed in the Oscar Howe Art Center in Mitchell.

A is for Artists
sharing pictures of their state
with pencil, paint, and canvas.
We marvel at what they create.

The Badlands area is a National Park. There are 244,000 acres of colorful rock formations, cliffs, spires, and prairie grasses.

Lakota Sioux called the region "*mako sica*," meaning "land bad." Nowadays a million people visit the Badlands each year to hike, camp, and enjoy the mysterious terrain.

Fifty miles west of the Badlands are the Black Hills, an area of low mountains. The hills are covered with pine forests, steep canyons, and huge rock formations. Harney Peak, South Dakota's highest point, is in the Black Hills. Caves, streams, national and state parks, museums, and wildlife bring millions of visitors to the Black Hills each year.

The Badlands and Black Hills are full of amazing sights. Exploring the world of nature in both areas shows us why one of South Dakota's slogans is "The Land of Infinite Variety."

B is for the Badlands and Black Hills.
In the western part of the state,
with tall pines, rocks, cliffs, and streams,
so much variety shows what nature creates.

South Dakota has always been known as a farming state. Corn, hay, oats, rye, sunflowers, soybeans, wheat, and alfalfa thrive in the rich black soil.

Open prairies make ranching important in South Dakota. About half of the state is pasture land, perfect for raising beef cattle, sheep, and hogs. Most of the ranches are west of the Missouri River, which divides the state into two sections: "East River" and "West River."

In 1892 the original Corn Palace was built in Mitchell. It was built to show off the farmers' harvests at a yearly fall festival. The outside of the Corn Palace is covered with murals each year made of multicolored corn, grains, grasses, and straw. South Dakota artists split each ear of corn in half and nail it in place to create the murals. The scenes illustrate life in South Dakota. Three thousand bushels of corn are used each year to decorate. The Corn Palace is sometimes called "the world's largest bird feeder."

C is for Corn Palace,
    all decked out with grains.
It will take you by surprise,
    so much grows under Dakota skies!

D is for De Smet,
the little town on the prairie
settled by the Ingalls family—
Pa and Ma, Laura, and Mary.

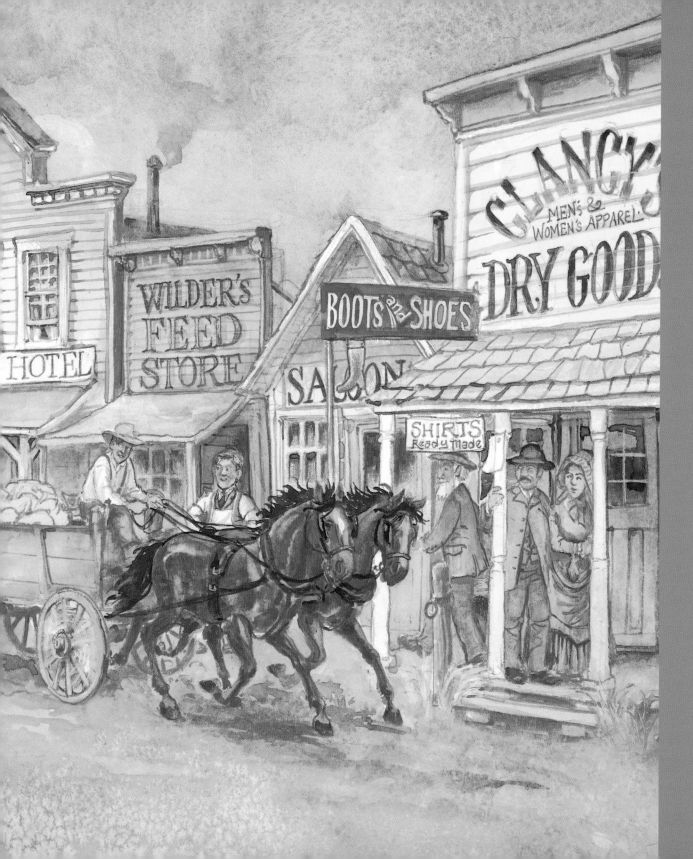

Dd

Laura Ingalls Wilder (1867–1957) is South Dakota's most famous author. In 1879 Charles and Caroline Ingalls (Pa and Ma) brought their daughters Laura, Mary, Carrie, and Grace to homestead near De Smet. Laura married Almanzo Wilder in 1885. The Wilders' daughter Rose was born on their farm in 1886. In 1894 Laura, Almanzo, and Rose moved to Mansfield, Missouri.

In 1932 Laura started her series of Little House books, telling of her pioneer life. The most famous book, *Little House on the Prairie*, became a television series. The books about De Smet are: *By the Shores of Silver Lake*, *The Long Winter*, *Little Town on the Prairie*, *These Happy Golden Years*, and *The First Four Years*.

Laura's books are translated into many languages. Her readers visit De Smet to see her homes, which are now museums. A pageant is held each summer which tells the story of the Ingalls family and other pioneers of De Smet. The town was named for a Belgian priest, Father Jean Pierre De Smet, who was an early missionary to the Sioux.

FORT CLATSOP

COLUMBIA RIVER

MARIAS RIVER

LEWIS

YELLOWSTONE RIVER

CLARK

E is for Expedition,
led by Lewis and Clark.
They traveled this state by boat and trails.
Their journals tell us exciting tales.

South Dakota was a part of the Louisiana Purchase, bought by the United States from France in 1803. This vast area was between the Mississippi River and the Rocky Mountains.

In 1804 President Thomas Jefferson named Meriwether Lewis and William Clark coleaders of an expedition to explore and map out the region from Missouri to the Pacific Ocean. With a crew of 45 people, they crossed South Dakota twice.

Lewis and Clark traveled by keelboat, following the Missouri River. Their journals tell of rich food sources on the prairie, wildlife, and river bluffs that seemed to be on fire. On August 30, 1804 Clark wrote of the speech-making, gift-giving, and smoking of peace pipes with the Yankton Sioux. This occurred on Calumet Bluff, near present-day Yankton, South Dakota.

Sacajawea, a Shosone, was the only woman on the Lewis and Clark journey. Six years after the expedition ended, Sacagawea died at Fort Manuel near Kenel, South Dakota.

Ee

F is for Flaming waters,
    bursting into fire and light.
        Have you ever seen burning water
    flickering bright all day and night?

The Flaming Fountain is in South Dakota's capital city, Pierre (pronounced "peer"). It honors South Dakotans who fought for their country. Water mixed with natural gas creates the ignited fountain. One of South Dakota's greatest heroes was Joe Foss (1915–2003). During World War II he was a top Marine ace pilot, shooting down 26 enemy planes. Later he was South Dakota's governor.

Pierre was named for an early fur trader, Pierre Chouteau. It was selected as South Dakota's capital in 1889. That's when Dakota Territory was divided into North Dakota and South Dakota. South Dakota was the 40th state admitted to the Union.

G is for the Glacial lakes
dotting the big wide prairie.
Dip into clear blue water.
Water sports are extraordinary!

Many of South Dakota's lakes were carved from the land thousands of years ago by glaciers. This left hundreds of lakes, mostly in the northeast part of the state. Dakota tribes once lived near these waters. Sica Hollow is in this region. Native Americans found this a mysterious place. They saw a stream of red water, glowing tree stumps, and heard moaning sounds in the wooded hollows.

Now the glacial lakes are great places for water sports and fishing. Walleye, the state fish, are found in most of the glacial lakes. Farther west is the Great Lakes region. Four dams along the Missouri River created the state's biggest lakes. They are Lake Oahe, Lake Francis Case, Lake Sharpe, and Lewis and Clark Lake.

H h

H is for Homestead
with houses made of sod.
Sodbusters used the Earth itself,
building homes you might think odd.

A house made of dirt? Yes, pioneers in South Dakota used grassy sod as "bricks" to build their homes. With few trees and lumber hard to get, this was a way to construct a house on a homestead, called a "soddie". Homesteads consisted of 160 acres. Any person over the age of 21 could file on a homestead. During the Great Dakota Land Boom in the 1880s settlers were called sodbusters.

Soddies were cool in summer, warm in winter. But they often needed repair. They leaked. Dirt trickled down the earthen walls. Creepy crawlers and snakes slithered in to visit. People replaced soddies with wooden houses as soon as they could. Today we can visit Prairie Homestead Historic Site near Badlands National Park. It is the only remaining soddie left from South Dakota's homesteading past. Homesteading was difficult, with crop failures, hard winters, drought, and grasshoppers.

I is for Immigrants
seeking South Dakota homes.
Long journeys from faraway
brought customs still thriving today.

Paleo-Indians are believed to be South Dakota's first people. They crossed into North America from Siberia on a land bridge around 8,000 B.C. and then migrated to South Dakota. Native Americans trace their roots in the state to the 1500s.

Today many South Dakotans are descended from European roots. Czechs, Germans, Scandinavians, Finns, Dutch, and Swiss immigrants arrived during the homestead era. They were lured by the promise of land and freedom. In the 1870s Hutterites started colonies in South Dakota. They live a communal, agricultural lifestyle.

The foreign-born worked hard adapting to prairie farming. They also retained customs from their old homes. Today South Dakota celebrates the heritage of the immigrants. Festivals like Czech Days in Tabor keep traditional food, music, crafts, and dancing alive. Rapid City's Stavkirke Church reminds us of Norway. It is a replica of a Norwegian place of worship, over 800 years old. In 2001 excavations in Deadwood revealed the location of Chinatown, which existed in the 1880s.

Ii

J is for Jewel Cave,
        filled with crystal gems,
glinting and shining as we explore.
        Can you find a passage not seen before?

J j

Jewel Cave is a national monument in the Black Hills, first discovered in 1900. Its 124 miles of mapped passageways make it the third-longest cave in the world. The cave was named for calcite crystals which cover the walls and ceilings. When lit they look like rooms full of diamonds. Stalactites, stalagmites, moonmilk, and other formations add to the beauty of Jewel Cave National Monument.

Hold onto your hat if you visit Wind Cave National Park near Hot Springs. Winds of 45 to 70 miles per hour may greet you at the entrance! There are seven other caves to visit in the Black Hills, making it truly "cave country."

K is for the "Buffalo King,"
who nurtured the wooly bison.
He saw the herd diminish
and saved it one by one.

James "Scotty" Philip became the "Buffalo King;" he worked to preserve dwindling bison populations of South Dakota. Today he would be called an animal rights advocate for his attempts to preserve wildlife. In the late 1800s just a few bison remained; Scotty bought a small herd. It grew to 900 and was the largest privately-owned herd in the world. More important, it assured the bison's future in South Dakota.

Scotty, who was an immigrant from Scotland, would be happy to know that South Dakota is now the state with the largest bison population. In Custer State Park alone, 1,400 bison roam freely. "Buffalo-jams" are common in the park when people stop their vehicles to wait for bison to cross the road.

K k

When the gold rush town of Deadwood was started in the 1870s it was populated by miners, gamblers, bad guys, and good guys. Some became legends. One was Wild Bill Hickok, a pioneer scout and crack pistol shot. He died from a bullet wound and is buried in Mount Moriah Cemetery. His friend Martha Jane Canary, nicknamed Calamity Jane, was a frontier woman often seen wearing buckskin. She was a heroine to some, once nursing Deadwood through a smallpox outbreak.

Others saw her as a tough, homeless woman. She asked to be "buried next to Wild Bill," and she was. Deadwood's first sheriff, Seth Bullock, put an end to some of the town's rowdiness. He, too, rests on Mount Moriah, along with Deadwood's colorful characters.

Early in Deadwood history, people longed for cats as mousers and pets. Phatty Thompson saw the need and filled it. He collected 50 cats in Wyoming and arrived in Deadwood with a wagonload of meowing passengers. Within an hour he sold them all for $1,000.

Modern day South Dakota legends include Tom Brokaw, broadcast journalist; Billy Mills, Olympic gold medalist; and Sparky Anderson, baseball player and team manager.

L is for Legends
 of Deadwood's gold rush past;
there's Wild Bill, Old Seth, and Calamity Jane,
 and a wagon full of cats.

SHERIFF

Sparky
Anderson

Wild Bill Hickok

Sitting Bull

Mount Rushmore

M is for Mount Rushmore,
carved with presidential faces.
Proud monument to democracy,
one of America's greatest places.

In 1927 sculptor Gutzon Borglum started a massive carving on the granite of Mount Rushmore, three miles from the mining town of Keystone. The project became one of South Dakota's—and America's—greatest monuments. Borglum, who was 60 when he started his work, envisioned the carving of four presidents. First, George Washington's face emerged as Father of the Nation. Next was Thomas Jefferson, who encouraged westward expansion. Theodore Roosevelt reminds us of his efforts in gaining justice for the workingman. And Abraham Lincoln is honored as the preserver of the Union.

The carving of Mount Rushmore cost almost a million dollars. Nearly 400 men worked on the mountain. They used dynamite, jackhammers, drills, and wedges. Cable cars took workers to the mountaintop, which is 5,675 feet above sea level. Carvers were suspended in cages and swing seats while working. Millions of people now visit Mount Rushmore yearly on visits to the Black Hills.

N is for Needles
reaching far into the sky.
Jagged spires of granite
and even a needle's eye!

Custer State Park, south of Mount Rushmore, is a place to view wildlife, mountain peaks, open grassland, lakes, and streams. The park was named for Colonel George Armstrong Custer who led an expedition into the Black Hills in 1874.

The Needles Highway meanders through the park for 14 miles. It has hairpin turns and granite tunnels. The name came from the tall, slender rock formations resembling needles. The Cathedral Spires region reminds us of a collection of church steeples.

Needle's Eye is one of Custer State Park's most unusual sights. Its smooth granite tower does look like "the eye of a needle"! Rock climbers are proud when they reach the top of the Needle's Eye; its smooth surface is hard to maneuver.

N
n

Oo

O is for Observation
    from satellites whirring in space.
Photos they capture from far above
        show us Earth's changing face.

EROS stands for Earth Resources Observation Systems. Its data center is located on the open prairie near Sioux Falls. EROS is part of the U.S. Geological Survey's National Mapping Division. Using a large satellite dish, the center receives transmissions from Earth orbiting satellites. Since it opened, EROS has stored, processed, and shared information, including aircraft and map data.

EROS is called the world's largest photo lab devoted to images of Earth taken from space. Archives house millions of images of land forms and aerial photographs. There are many uses of the images EROS processes and stores. Scientists and mapmakers use EROS to explain both natural and man-made disasters on Earth. Floods on America's rivers, hurricanes, the Valdez oil spill, the eruption of Mount St. Helens, and the Iraqi War can all be studied at EROS.

You can tour EROS and see how Earth looks from above; maybe you will spot your own hometown!

South Dakota winters are known for their bone-chilling temperatures, blinding snowstorms, and wild winds. During the homesteading era blizzards were dangerous to early settlers, isolating them from supplies and help. Today blizzards can still stop all traffic and create many hazards.

After long, cold winters the first sign of spring on the prairie is the pasque flower. It grows all over the state and is a member of the buttercup family. The pasque is South Dakota's state flower. Other state symbols include the state bird, a Chinese ringneck pheasant; the state tree, Black Hills Spruce; and the state insect, the honeybee.

South Dakota's state nickname is "The Mount Rushmore State."

P p

P is for Pasque flower
which makes a lavender bouquet.
Its appearance says winter's over
and spring's on the way!

In 1874 gold was discovered in the Black Hills. The news spread like wild-fire and prospectors flocked to Dakota Territory. The richest deposits were between the present towns of Lead and Deadwood. Deadwood became the center of mining operations. Some miners became rich overnight. Others gave up, sold their claims, and moved on. Still others lost their riches gambling in rowdy mining camps.

The Black Hills were sacred territory to the Sioux. They called the area "*paha sapa*." The stampede in their lands led to uprisings led by Sitting Bull and Crazy Horse. In 1876 the Sioux signed a treaty giving up claims in the Black Hills. Most of the Native Americans settled on reservations west of the Missouri River.

Gold mining in the Black Hills continued until World War II. Homestake Mine in Lead, America's largest producing gold mine, closed in 2000.

Q is for Quest
for glittering nuggets of gold,
bringing miners to the Black Hills—
fortunes found, lost, and sold.

Almost half of South Dakota is covered with open pastures. West of the Missouri River, the West River region is where most ranching occurs. The grasslands make ideal homes for cattle and sheep. Because of drier weather than in the East River area, grass looks brown most of the year. The 1990 movie *Dances with Wolves* was filmed at the Triple U Buffalo Ranch; it won an Academy Award.

Beef cattle ranchers brand their calves born in the spring with a hot iron to show who owns them. They graze until fall when they are rounded up to be sold. Then they are fattened and sold again to be slaughtered for meat. In good weather the cattle graze on the miles and miles of growing grass. When snow covers the ground, ranchers carry feed to their herds and spread it on the ground for eating.

South Dakota is also sheep country. Most sheep also range west of the Missouri River. South Dakota is a leader in wool production.

R is for Ranching
on miles of open plains
sheep and cattle graze,
roaming grassy terrains.

S s

S is for Sioux,
the natives of the state.
Dakota, Lakota, and Nakota,
each has stories and culture great.

South Dakota is home of the Sioux Nation. It consists of three bands, Dakota, Lakota, and Nakota. Each spoke its own dialect. They originally migrated from Minnesota's lakes and woodlands. The Sioux dominated the northern plains by the end of the eighteenth century. They followed the buffalo herds that gave them their livelihood. A Sioux legend tells of the Great Spirit appearing in the form of a buffalo to feed his starving people.

The Sioux Nation had no written language but preserved its culture through storytelling. Drawings on animal hides recorded tribal events. Four virtues became important to the Sioux. They are: "*woksape*" (wisdom), "*woohitika*" (bravery), "*wowacintanka*" (fortitude), and "*wacantognaka*" (generosity).

Arrival of settlers in Dakota Territory made Sioux life difficult. A treaty in 1868 created the Great Sioux Reservation. Today there are more than 62,000 Native Americans in South Dakota.

Powwows, art, and celebrations remind us of Sioux traditions today.

T is for Triceratops,
the fossil of this state.
Buried bones now turned to stones
that diggers excavate.

Triceratops lived in South Dakota 68 million years ago. It was a horned dinosaur. Today South Dakota shows us much about archaeology and paleontology. Mammoth Site near Hot Springs is one of the world's largest exhibits of fossils. The spot was a sinkhole where wooly mammoths came to drink. When they could not get out, they died of starvation. Fifty fossils are on display.

In 1990 the most complete Tyrannosaurus rex skeleton was unearthed. It was sold at auction for $8 million. Another T-rex, nicknamed "Stan," is now in the Black Hills Museum of Natural History in Hill City.

Archaeological digs in South Dakota are constantly in progress.

T t

U is for USS *South Dakota*—
heroic battleship of World War II,
fighting through Atlantic and Pacific
to preserve world peace for me and you.

U
u

The battleship USS *South Dakota* is proudly remembered for its service during World War II. It was launched in 1941, the year America entered the war. In the Pacific the ship was involved in the Guadalcanal Campaign and the Battle of the Santa Cruz Islands. Japanese bombers hit the ship twice, and other damages made major repairs necessary. In 1943–1944 the ship operated in the Atlantic and then returned to the Pacific, where she was again bombed. During an air attack the ship's guns downed 32 enemy planes. It also destroyed three Japanese cruisers.

The USS *South Dakota* was in Tokyo Bay when the Japanese surrendered in 1945. The ship and its crew were heroes of World War II. It was said that "USS *South Dakota* can take it and it can dish it out."

The ship was decommissioned and sold for scrap in 1962. But it was never forgotten. In Sioux Falls the USS *South Dakota* Memorial reminds us of the brave ship.

Francois and Louis-Joseph La Verendrye were the first European explorers to visit South Dakota. In 1743 they buried a lead plate near present-day Fort Pierre. The plate claimed the region for France and also proved that the French brothers were there. In 1762 France gave its land west of the Mississippi River to Spain. Spain returned it to France in 1800. In 1803 the area became American.

Fort Pierre was the oldest non-Native American settlement in South Dakota. A fur trading post was started on the banks of the Missouri River in 1817. History forgot the Verendryes' lead plate until 1913. Imagine the excitement when three schoolchildren unearthed it! The South Dakota State Historical Society now owns the first written record of a visit to the state.

V is for Verendrye,
    two brothers with that name.
French explorers with a goal—
    a lead plate made their claim.

In 1931 Ted and Dorothy Hustead put up a highway sign saying "FREE ICE WATER, WALL DRUG." Their tiny drugstore in Wall was soon filled with thirsty travelers coming from the Badlands or heading to the Black Hills. Signs along the highway now lure millions of people to the Husteads' store, which has grown to mammoth proportions.

You can still buy medicine at Wall Drug, but it is also filled with shops, restaurants, wildlife exhibits, an art gallery, singing mechanical cowboys, and more. Native American crafts, rock shops, Western clothing, and 6,000 pairs of cowboy boots also fill the huge emporium. Exhibits explain South Dakota history.

The Hustead family still operates Wall Drug. The cold, clear ice water is always free.

W is for Wall Drug—
world's largest drugstore.
Bursting with things to buy
and treasures to explore.

X marks the spot
of the center of the nation.
You can leave your footprint there
on a South Dakota vacation.

Imagine looking east or west, north or south, and knowing you are in the exact center of the United States! Only in South Dakota can you do this. A location 23 miles north of Belle Fourche is the geographical center of the United States. A stone monument explains this fact. The center point has been a moveable one. For many years the center of the nation was near Smith Center, Kansas. But when Alaska and Hawaii were added to the Union in 1957 and 1959, a change had to be made. Through mathematical wizardry the new site was established and shifted to South Dakota. The United States spreads out equally to the four corners of the compass from its South Dakota center.

Y is for York—
traveler with Lewis and Clark.
He amazed the friendly Sioux
who never saw skin so dark.

William Clark, coleader of the Lewis and Clark Expedition, brought along his servant York for the journey. York was the first African American to see South Dakota. York's name often appeared in Clark's journal. While hunting for goats and prairie dogs (called "barking squirrels"), Clark and York spotted a herd of at least 500 buffalo. York killed two of them.

The Native Americans were fascinated with the African American. York was a celebrity. Clark wrote in his journal: "Those Indians were much astonished at my Servant. They never saw a black man before, all flocked around him and examined him from top to toe."

Y
y

Z is for Ziolkowski—
a sculptor of many skills.
His massive carving of Crazy Horse
gazes at the Black Hills.

Seventeen miles from Mount Rushmore is a fifth face on a mountain. It is Crazy Horse, selected by Lakota leaders for his pride and courage. In 1948 they asked sculptor and artist Korczak Ziolkowski for a carving of their hero. Korczak started the face of Crazy Horse with drills and explosives. His work was a nonprofit, lifelong goal. Eventually Crazy Horse became a family project, including the sculptor's wife Ruth and their 10 children. After Korczak's death in 1982, the family continued his dream. In 1998 Crazy Horse's face was complete. It was as tall as a nine-story building.

Nearly eight million tons of granite have been blasted away from the mountain. The Crazy Horse Memorial is the largest sculpture in the world. When finished, it will be taller than the Washington Monument. With outstretched arm, Crazy Horse will ride his horse into the skies.

Each year in June the annual Crazy Horse Volksmarch is held. The hike allows people to walk to Crazy Horse's arm for a broad view of the Sioux's sacred Black Hills.

Monumental Facts from the Mount Rushmore State

1. Which South Dakota artist specialized in painting the lives of pioneers?

2. The Native Americans are important to South Dakota history. Which tribe was living on the prairie when settlers first arrived in the state?

3. Which native South Dakota mammal was saved from extinction?

4. Who described South Dakota pioneer life in her many books?

5. There are two separate mountain carvings in the Black Hills. Which one honors a brave Sioux hero?

6. Which long river divides South Dakota into two parts, East River and West River?

7. Can you name the four presidents whose faces are carved on Mount Rushmore?

8. Which dinosaur's bones were discovered buried in South Dakota?

9. The most important exploration through South Dakota happened in 1804. Who were the leaders of this expedition?

10. Many lakes dot the prairie landscape of South Dakota. Fishing is good; what is the state fish?

11. What highly prized mineral was discovered in the Black Hills in 1874?

12. EROS, located in South Dakota, does important work for America. What is the job of EROS?

13. What animal was imported to the town of Deadwood soon after it was founded?

14. Why is South Dakota one-half of a larger territory?

15. Do you know what South Dakota's capital city is named?

16. Although much of South Dakota is prairie land, the Black Hills are covered with trees. What is the state tree?

17. Why do cattle and sheep thrive in South Dakota?

18. What well-known business got its start by giving away ice water?

19. How can you be in the middle of America in South Dakota?

20. How do we know that French explorers passed through South Dakota in the 1700s?

Answers

1. Harvey Dunn (1884-1952).

2. The Sioux.

3. The buffalo, which now wander freely through Custer State Park.

4. Laura Ingalls Wilder's Little House books tell us about homesteading in South Dakota.

5. Crazy Horse, which will be the world's largest mountain carving when it is finished.

6. The Missouri River flows through the state. It makes an unofficial boundary between the east and west portions of the state.

7. Washington, Jefferson, Theodore Roosevelt, and Lincoln.

8. Triceratops, which lived there millions of years ago.

9. Lewis and Clark.

10. The Walleye.

11. Gold.

12. EROS collects photos of Earth taken from space.

13. Cats were brought to Deadwood.

14. Originally the state was called Dakota Territory. When South Dakota became a state in 1889, the land to the north became North Dakota.

15. Pierre.

16. The Black Hills Spruce.

17. The land is flat and covered with grass; perfect for grazing!

18. Wall Drug, in the town of Wall.

19. The geographical center of the United States is in South Dakota.

20. The explorers buried an engraved lead plate. It was discovered over 200 years later.

William Anderson

William Anderson is delighted to write about South Dakota, where his ancestors pioneered in the 1880s. A century later he helped restore Laura Ingalls Wilder's South Dakota homes, and received the state's Robinson Award for historical writing. His books include: *Laura Ingalls Wilder: A Biography*; *River Boy*: *The Story of Mark Twain*; and *The World of the Trapp Family*. In 2002 he was invited to Laura Bush's White House conference on the frontier.

As a speaker, William Anderson has traveled across America. But his favorite summers were spent in South Dakota. His home is in Michigan, where he teaches and writes. Visit him online at www.williamandersonbooks.com.

Cheryl Harness

Since her childhood in California, Cheryl's life has been influenced by books about Laura and Mary Ingalls and Tom Sawyer and Huck Finn. She received her art-education degree from Central Missouri State University and her first job was as a theme park portrait artist. She has also designed paper goods for Hallmark and Current, and has created needlework kits and music boxes. She's sculpted, sewn (and worn) period costumes, and written and/or illustrated more than 30 picture books. Find out about these, as well as her first, soon-to-be-published novel at www.cherylharness.com.

Cheryl lives outside the Queen City of the Trails: Independence, Missouri, with her Scottie, Maude, and two cats: Elizabeth and Merrie Emma.